A Cultural Change

Floor Support has been developed with the purpose of bridging the gap between Training and Business Operations that inevitably exists. The education from New Hire Training quickly fades with day-to-day experience and the forming of new habits. Floor Support provides the much needed one-on-one contact and continuous training that is necessary for efficacious quality improvements.

"KNOWLEDGE IS POWER ONLY WHEN IT IS SHARED!"
DAWAINE CASSIDY

D. Cassidy and J. Hagey
Life Academy of Learning

Content

About the Authors

Dawaine Cassidy is a husband and a father who has learned through the support of a loving family to balance his personal life and his profession. This has brought him so much personal strength and desire to share the knowledge that he has gained. He has developed and managed a technical training program at Universal Studios Orlando (Universal). He was with Universal for 16 years. He started out as an order picker in the their offsite warehouse and worked and networked his way to his last assignment which was overseeing and developing the technical training program for the Wizarding World of Harry Potter at Universals Islands Of Adventure theme park. He is a graduate student with a Master's Degree in Business Administration, and Human Resources Management. His desire is to share his knowledge that he has gained with the hope that it may help those that are striving to accomplish their goals and overcome any opposition they may face. He believes if we apply what we learn from our challenges he will be strengthened and future success will be ours.

Jason Hagey believes we are all much more likely to act our way into a new way of thinking than to think our way into a new way of acting. He has 15+ years of management and consulting experience developing or nurturing cultures for positive, continuous, quality improvements. Jason is passionate about the potential of the individual and the organizations in which they work. Having worked in numerous industries and with businesses in all phases of the business cycle, he uniquely understands business operations, training, and management at many levels.

This book is designed with a singular purpose: help you structure a continuous improvement culture in your customer service organization.

Customer service organizations often suffer from stagnation. Producing continuous improvement is often just a program or an initiative – like the flavor-of-the-month – and usually disappears after some focus group discussions occur and some plans are put into place. The reason that continuous improvement doesn't usually go beyond just an initiative is because continuous improvement isn't a program. Continuous improvement must be built into the culture. For an organization to really develop into what it's capable of, continuous improvement is required but that improvement must be culturally-based. For a *customer service* organization to really develop into what it's capable of, a culture which fosters continuous improvement is required.

Do you have a vision for your customer service organization? Do you know what you want to accomplish? Have you ever really looked at your culture – really looked at it – to see what it's made of and what it needs in order to become the kind of organization it can be? Should be?

In the following pages we will talk about our philosophy at the 'Life Academy of Learning' (the backbone behind why and how we do what we do) and then how to apply that

philosophy to structure your customer service organization to grow and develop into a continuous improvement culture. If you will follow the simple guidelines that we give you – keeping the philosophy in mind – you will find awesome improvement in your organization and the kind of growth that you have desired for you and the individuals you work with.

LIFE ACADEMY OF LEARNING: OUR PHILOSOPHY

AN INTRODUCTION

Welcome to the Life Academy of Learning. Here at the Academy the belief is that life is our classroom. The three main areas of focus that are keys to future success are as follows:

Life Decisions | Educational Decisions | Career Decisions

Each area of focus plays an integral part in the other two. The hierarchy starts with Life Decisions and ends up with Career Decisions being the ultimate goal. Many times life sends us in a different direction and when that happens often there is no rhyme or reason – or so we think. Each experience in life is there to teach us something. It is up to us to find those gems in amongst the confusion and, many times, pains of life. Realizing that we are all pupils is vital but remember, even the greatest intellectual giant kicks against the simplest bricks if they choose not to apply what has been learned from past experiences.

Life is to be learned from. That's a simple statement that many of us forget. Or, if we remember that we are to learn from this life we have struggles learning from our experiences. After all, how many times have you wondered why you keep doing the same things? How many times have you asked yourself, "Why do I keep doing this?" Life is to be learned from, but the lessons aren't always easy to learn. We're engrained with biases, habits, and other prejudices that have influenced the way we think. Also, how should we learn from life? What framework should we be using to improve our lives?

There is a constant barrage of ideas about success and successful living. We have all manner of books and articles, memes and quotes thrust at us through our media, all with the purpose of teaching us to think successfully, look at life with successful eyes. But how much do we actual know of putting those things into action? Often we are given 'positive thoughts' and aphorisms to base our life on. These definitely have their place and are necessary to keep an outlook of motivation and inspiration. And, often, we know what we should be doing - real estate, investments, working harder or smarter, being entrepreneurial, finding our niche, innovating, finding our creative side or passion, etc. - but we can't bring ourselves to do these things. Perhaps all things can be boiled down to one thought: do it. Or, as Nike proposed for so many years: Just Do It. But doing it (whatever 'it' is) isn't as easy to do. As in many things, it's easy to say and much harder to put into practice. And being successful in life usually ends up being in accomplishments and achievements rather than in the journey, despite those motivational statements of success being in the journey or the continual pursuit of a worthwhile ideal. After all, we do want to accomplish something in our relatively short lives; we want to leave a mark on the world - hopefully a mark for good. As Ayn Rand put it, "To make my life a reason unto itself. I know what I want up to the age of two hundred. Know what you want in life and go after it."

We each have our differing beliefs in what 'good' really is and what 'success' must be in order to feel successful in our lives. This is understandable. We are each individuals. Our perspectives on life, love, and the fruits of happiness are ours alone. And, we all have the choice of how we want to accomplish the end results of our lives. We may not be able to control our circumstances, though there are many philosophies that tell us we can at least influence those circumstances, but we have the ability to control our perception of those circumstances - always. As is often said, we have control of our attitude.

Life is to be learned from. Whether you believe in an afterlife or not, evolution or not, learning is inherent in the nature of our beings. Becoming better, growing and developing throughout life, is the pursuit that many feel as a deep instinct. Life is our classroom, our academy, for learning. How well we learn from life is dependent on many factors, all of which come back to our perceptions of reality, our attitude, and how we go about learning from life. The motivational quotes and inspirational stories all help us to frame our attitudes and influence our perceptions of life, the universe, and everything. They are important and worthy of our emulation. Just doing it is important - there must be action to learn.

In the world of education, there are many philosophies, methodologies, and approaches to curriculum. Human beings have put a great deal of effort into understanding these things because we know that there are better ways to learn than others. We apply these things to formal learning, but why haven't we applied a framework to learning from life?

There are many ways to learn from life. There are at least as many frameworks for learning from life as there are educational philosophies. And, some approaches work better for some than others. It is in this spirit that the authors and creators of 'Life Academy of Learning' present our perspective to learning from life. We know it may not be the best approach for everyone, but we desire to help as many as we can in improving their lives as we can and we believe that we have found an approach that benefits many - and we would like to share that approach with you.

To explain our approach to life learning, we will borrow from different fields of study to give depth and understanding (transference) to our explanations.

EMOTIONAL PHYSICS

EMOTION

Regarding the word 'emotion,' there is a distinction between emotion and the result of the emotion (i.e. behaviors and emotional expressions). People often behave in certain ways as a direct result of their emotional state. We respond to life based on how we feel more than how we think.

PHYSICS

Physics is a natural science that involves the study of matter and its motion through space and time, as well as all applicable concepts, including energy and force.

More broadly, it is a general analysis of nature conducted to understand how the universe behaves.

EMOTIONAL PHYSICS

Emotional Physics becomes, therefore, the study of behavioral actions based on the decision making process within an individual as they apply what they internally learned from external influences. This is done throughout that individual's life. Put simply, we study our actions and the decisions that led us to that end result – and we learn from that experience.

To best understand our actions and the decision that led to that end result we must understand specific principles. Our understanding of the energy and forces that we experience requires us to understand what we are looking for in our introspective study. To better lay this foundation, we require an understanding of the Laws of Growth.

THE LAWS OF GROWTH

From our earliest years in school, when studying Natural Science we were taught to think of Sir Isaac Newton and his Laws of Motion. His findings were first published in July 5, 1687. His Laws have been used countless times since then. Through his findings, Newton was able to give an explanation to the workings of physical objects and systems.

Using Newton's Laws of Motion as a pattern for discussion and framework for principles, we propose to give an explanation to the workings of spiritual, emotional, and mental 'objects' and systems. The following Laws of Growth are our contribution to framing how we learn from experience. Learning comes when one is in a state of rest, ponders experience, and applies that knowledge to action. To prove one's learning one must be exposed to forces to challenge each principle and prove its integrity and worth. Growth is the result of this continued process. The absence of growth leads to internal obscurity, and this detachment leads to confusion.

To avoid confusion, and the internal obscurity that leads to that confusion, we must understand how growth is accomplished. Growth requires that energies and the forces of our learning push forward. We cannot be stagnate in our experience of life. Think of life in this analogy: we are on roller skates heading up a steep hill. It takes moving forward consistently with continual energy and force to propel us up the hill. At times we must contemplate, but we must keep moving, in a lowered state of energy and force, but we cannot stop our forward momentum. As with any roller skater going up a hill, to stop means going backward. We lose energy and momentum. The force of our efforts becomes negatively impacted. In that, we lose progress in our journey. So it is with growth.

When we stagnate, we gain a void in our learning - a gap - and this causes an internal obscurity. Obscurity is a kind of vacuum, and there is darkness in that vacuum. In other words, it is the absence of light. Learning has often been compared to the illumination of the mind, the soul. We believe that all intelligence is compared to light because when we learn to 'see' we grow, and we can only see when we have light. Our perspective is clearer with better light. Our perspective is diminished when we lack light. Just as we have troubles orienting ourselves in a dark room, we have troubles seeing (and therefore learning) when our minds and souls are dark. It's easy to be confused and disoriented in darkness. And not being able to see means that we cannot grow.

LAWS OF GROWTH DEFINED

The Laws of Growth consist of three principles that form the foundation for Emotional Physics. Each describes a force we experience as we make life's choices. The three laws are as follows:

First Law: Personal Stagnation. Every individual remains in a constant state of denial by rejection of the enlightenment obtained through experiences. The result is a negative outlook and ignorance.

Second Law: Individual Illumination. An individual is subjected to acceptance and implementation of internal learning based on influence and experiences of external forces in life. The more that this process is applied, growth increases and internal obscurity is diminished.

Third Law: Mutual Edification. Two or more individuals participate in the mutual exchange of enlightenment with different points of view. As the individuals discuss their points of view in equity and respect, they diminish confusion and develop new growth. This does not mean that they necessarily agree, but their understanding of their own learning and the learning of others fosters the improvement of all involved.

INTERNAL COMPASS

The Internal Compass is an internal navigational 'device' based on intellectual skill and proven tools. If used properly, one can navigate through challenges and obtain unforeseen success.

We add to your Life Academy of Learning 'vocabulary' this idea of the internal compass because we believe that you can only grow from what you know now. Your context for the current moment is where you will start your decision-making process. If you understand where you stand today, if you know what you have in intellect and tools, then you can grow from a foundation. If you approach life without understanding that you have something to stand on already, then you begin in a vacuum – personal stagnation – and your results will match. Learning to go with your previous learning is all part of navigating through challenges. If you doubt all that you know, you will know very little in the end. Knowing very little will lead to continual stagnation. Know this: you know enough now to get started on your journey to improving yourself and your organization.

CONTINUOUS IMPROVEMENT: MUTUAL EDIFICATION

Our philosophy builds from the idea of mutual edification. In this book you will find information (a point of view) regarding our years of experience with structuring continuous improvement cultures in customer service environments. Sharing our perspective, we hope to give you our enlightenment and help you develop improvement in your organization. We have found that human resources – the most important resource we have – are best improved by improving the organization at an individual level. This individual education begins with having alignment and structure, developing on the idea of accountability, consistency, and mutual purpose. Therefore, we give you an idea of alignment and structure that will greatly benefit your organization if it's implemented and followed through.

Not only has this philosophy produced this book, but it is built on every concept of education and improvement that we know. For instance, the structure for fostering improvement is built on a model that requires your organization to exchange information: mutual edification. Your organization will grow in skill and abilities that will lead to better execution on all company objectives as it discovers knowledge and learns to communicate that information throughout the organization. This growth begins with developing a mission and vision to align with, followed by a structure that supports those objectives stated by the organization. The mission and vision should not be a company-only practice, but should be implemented at every level, in every department, and all teams. Below is an example of the 'Floor Support' mission and vision that works in improving customer service organizations. We have included sample guiding principles and goals so that you can understand how best to implement your own 'Floor Support.'

THE ANSWER: FLOOR SUPPORT

The answer to customer service continuous improvement begins with a concept we call 'Floor Support.' Floor Support is a leadership-centric structure that builds confidence in your organization and fosters growth and continual development. This is the framework for continuous improvement. We try to teach our concepts through the actual implementation of Floor Support, so our examples will all be about

Floor Support, though these concepts can be used for much more than Floor Support alone. Because most Floor Support will come from your training department, we have included job descriptions for both Floor Support and Classroom Training and how they would be structured *interchangeably*.

The structure of Floor Support can be used by trainers, managers, supervisors, or within the ranks of customer service representatives. The structure has been outlined here with a training team in mind, but it's very agile for any business. The ideas remain the same, though the personnel that fill the positions may be different for every organization. Also, the titles are obviously flexible to meet company needs. The idea here is that you have built a structure (formal or informal) that fosters a culture of continuous improvement.

For instance, one place we have used this structure is to build an informal organization within a department of trainers. The call center we were in was very large (1600+ seats) and required an entire team of trainers to do several months of new hire training. After this training was over, we still had the personnel but they lacked purpose and structure. The group could have been disbanded at this point, but with the establishment of continuous improvement as a goal, rather than creating an initiative or program, the new hire training team was given this Floor Support structure and a purpose was developed for the group.

Up-trainings were, of course, devised, but there is always the need to improve through coaching and to support in answering questions. The training team became Floor Support. Though there were no pay raises for the different responsibilities it created an atmosphere of accountability and consistency that was sorely needed in a call center and raised the level of responsibility amongst the trainers. The result was greater cohesion in CSR understanding of company processes and procedures, better accountability for up-trainings, and a coaching program that fostered continuous improvement across the organization. Manager and supervisors looked to the Floor Support group for virtually everything because they knew that the whole organization was lifted.

In another call center (300+ seats), Floor Support was developed to answer questions and provide internal support from within the ranks of the CSRs themselves. Though they were a smaller group of CSRs, the diversity of their needs (product support, sales support, technical support, shipping/returns, etc.) required experts in the various areas and 24 hour support. Again, no raises were given, just added *opportunity* to grow and an increase in ownership. Thus, Floor Support not only incorporated a structure of teams, but the teams were based upon expertise and were scheduled according to the amount of support necessary at any hour of the day. The result was a call center that had a second tier of support, CSRs seeking to become better at their jobs because they could be added to this group of Floor Support, and an entire pool of leadership to pull from when the time came to hire for supervisors and other management positions.

To implement these ideas as fast as possible, we've included here the following:

- A Sample Floor Support Mission and Vision, Guiding Principles and Purpose
- An Organizational Chart Template for Floor Support
- What the Career Development Plan is regarding Floor Support and its structure
- An Example of how the Floor Support Organizational Chart would look when in practice (based on an actual training group)
- Floor Support and Classroom Training Job Descriptions so you will know what needs to happen at every level of the structure and at every phase of the organization
- Documents that have proven useful in tracking and developing the organization

IN THE BEGINNING: AN ORGANIZATION'S MISSION, VISION, GUIDING PRINCIPLES, AND PURPOSE

Every organization needs to have purpose and systems that are built to accomplish that purpose.

Whether your organization is a call center or a retail outlet, you need to set forth the direction of your business. The following are quick and easy definitions of what you need to get started in fostering a continuous improvement culture: Mission, Vision, Guiding Principles, and Purpose.

A mission statement identifies an organization's primary *reason for being* and its distinctive competency.

A vision statement identifies an organization's "envisioned future" – the largest, most grandiose goal – which may be entirely impossible to reach but the "mountain you want to climb."

The Guiding Principles guide the culture. These principles help to define who should be on the team and the expectations that management has for their performance.

- If you were to start a new organization, would you build it around this core value/behavior regardless of the industry?
- Would you want your organization to continue to stand for this core value/behavior 100 years into the future, no matter what changes occur in the outside world?
- Do you believe that those who do not share this core value/behavior, those who breach it

consistently, simply do not belong in your organization?

Purpose is the desired outcomes. They begin as the overall objectives of an organization and should be strategic in nature. They can also be summarized in a set of key performance indicators, which measure on-going performance. To see how these principles work in practice, the following example has been outlined for Floor Support.

SAMPLE FLOOR SUPPORT MISSION AND VISION

OUR MISSION

Our mission is to deliver high-quality education and coaching solutions that are relevant, innovative, timely and affordable – striving to consistently exceed consumer expectations.

OUR VISION

Our vision is to disseminate information and deliver solutions that enhance quality and improve efficiency in evolving business operations.

OUR GUIDING PRINCIPLES

- Integrity
- Respect
- Trust
- Teamwork
- Positivity
- Confidence
- Responsibility
- Passion
- Humility
- Execution

OUR PURPOSE

Floor Support has been developed with the purpose of bridging the gap between Classroom Training and Business Operations that inevitably exists. The education from New Hire Training quickly fades with day-to-day experience and the forming of new habits. While Supervisors and Managers take care of administrative and team needs their influence in hands-on improvement is spread thin with their many responsibilities. 'Floor Support' provides the much needed one-on-one contact and continuous training that is necessary for efficacious quality improvements. Floor Support is meant to be the "best friend" to Management and to support their initiatives for the quickest and most personal improvements possible.

The focus of Floor Support is on needs assessment, root cause analysis, and providing solutions to close the gaps that inevitably exist between training and real-world application. When done properly, Floor Support improves customer service performance dramatically as a catalyst for excellence in exceeding consumer expectations. These changes will optimize productivity, improve employee satisfaction and enhance consumer experience.

- Increase operational efficiency by increasing first contact resolution and optimizing problem-solving.
- Improve consumer experience by understanding the consumer/operations experience and developing customer service competencies.
- Reduce risk and avoid unnecessary costs of penalties associated with program non-compliance.

FLOOR SUPPORT STRUCTURE AND CAREER DEVELOPMENT PLANS

The following Organizational Chart Template was developed with the belief that to get things done there must be an intelligent structure for work. Also, the organizational system was designed with the intent to give Floor Support the opportunity to improve their abilities, expand their skillsets, and capitalize on personal motivations to improve and grow in their jobs. With each position is a raise in opportunity for growth and responsibility in the organization – that doesn't necessitate an increase in wages.

There are five levels of Floor Support and an additional support position:

- Floor Trainer
- Team Lead
- Shift Lead
- Floor Lead
- Development Supervisor

The additional support position is the Communications and Current Operations (CCO) Trainer who exists as a direct report to the Training Supervisor. Job Descriptions for all these positions are found later.

Every Floor Trainer develops with their Team Lead (every Team Lead with Shift Lead, and Shift Lead with Floor Lead, etc.) an Individual Development Plan (IDP). The IDP is composed of personal activities and skills development necessary for the individual to progress from their current status to the next, up the leadership pipeline. IDP activities are determined based on individual goals and the goals of the organization. Where the individual and organization meet, the IDP addresses opportunities for growth. The purpose is to engage Floor Trainers in work that is personally meaningful to them.

The Career Development Plan addresses organizational growth and accountability. The IDP addresses personal growth and accountability. Both give a structure to activities that need accomplishment. In this way, Floor Support can be effective in disseminating education and in 'getting things done.' Activities for Floor Support to accomplish are defined by performance gaps.

Performance gaps are identified through a process of needs assessment and a root cause analysis (Hit List) and solutions are identified and assignments given (Task List) to provide Floor Support. Floor Trainers are given directions based on the 'Hit List' developed from needs assessment and root cause analysis. The Hit List is a list of actionable intelligence. When Floor Trainers work with Customer Service Representatives (CSRs), trends in poor habits will be recognized. These trends will be seen as Floor Trainers use the 'Current Forms' found at the end of this document and other tools yet to be developed. As trends are established, a Hit List of items will emerge.

From the Hit List, the trending in performance gaps is identified in collaboration between Floor Trainers and their Team Leads, again between Team Leads and Shift Leads, and finally at the level of Floor Lead and Training Supervisor. As trends are identified, a 'Task List' is developed. The Task List is a specific list, by priority, of activities that must be accomplished and to whom assignments are given in order to get things done. This Task List ranges in responsibility between Floor Trainer and Development Supervisor, depending on the level of need. For example, if the Task List item is composed of something that needs to be addressed at an individual CSR level, then Floor Trainers will be given specific assignments to get this Task List item done. Additionally, if the Task List item is something that needs to be addressed with Senior Management, then the Training Supervisor will be the one assigned. Coordination of activities necessitates leadership and accountability through the Floor Support ranks and this is where Team, Floor and Floor Lead leadership steps in. The nature of Task List assignments will depend on what needs to be done as a solution to the Hit List items.

FLOOR SUPPORT JOB DESCRIPTIONS

As a reiteration, Floor Support doesn't have to be about trainers – it can be from any rankings within the customer service environment (e.g. managers, supervisors, or CSRs). The structure gives direction and purpose to each individual and requires accountability throughout the organization. As this is put into place, the whole culture becomes about continuous improvement.

Clarity of individual purpose requires that everyone in the organization knows what they are supposed to do. This is especially true when implementing Floor

Support into your customer service environment. The following are basic job descriptions (to modify or add to according to your organization). The structure's job descriptions are necessary for Career Development Plans to work in tandem with one another. These Floor Support incorporate a training perspective into the Floor Support Career Development Plans, but it can be modified to fit whatever your needs are. Being in the 'job' means that the individual receives personal illumination; the opportunity to learn and implement enhances their growth and understanding of personal purpose.

Between the structure and the opportunities of each position, there is an inherent boost in the leadership quality that begins to derive from everyone actively working to help the other to improve. The purposes behind these different 'jobs' is as much for the leader as it is for those who follow them. It's a learning organization that you are building. It is not about 'authority' or 'being higher up' but the structure is built on the idea of servant leadership: we are each here to serve one another. In fact, if you so desire, you can periodically reassign positions throughout the year. This would allow those who have followed to have opportunity to learn and grow from those who now follow them, and those who once led to follow and learn from the experience of those whom they previously served. The mutual enlightenment that occurs helps the entire organization to grow in skills and abilities.

FLOOR TRAINER

Floor Trainers leverage knowledge and relationships to understand the training and development needs of Business Operations personnel and work to meet those needs through support, individual coaching, and team trainings. Floor Trainers are responsible for building positive relationships with Managers, Supervisors and Customer Service Representatives. Floor Trainers draft reports and communicate findings and analysis with Training Management. Floor Trainers perform day-to-day delivery, administration, interpretation and compliance of learning programs according to established policies and procedures. Floor Trainers support the continuous improvement of their functional area through development and implementation of learning programs. With guidance, Floor Trainers provide expertise, support and advice to Managers, Supervisors and Customer Service Representatives and other management teams. Floor Trainers serve on cross functional teams and share best practices. Floor Trainers conduct Root Cause Analysis and Needs Assessments.

FLOOR SUPPORT TEAM LEAD

Team Leads are responsible for supporting, coaching, and leading a team of Floor Trainers. Team Leads partner with Floor Support Staff to ensure training compliance is met. Team Leads collaborate with Operations staff to meet training goals and implement operational changes to enhance effectiveness. Team Leads continuously train Floor Trainers on all training updates. Team Leads conduct, direct and lead training and related developmental activities needed to support operational objectives in support of the Operations staff and Training Management. Team Leads oversee and coordinate the work of assigned Floor Trainers throughout Business Operations. Team Leads are responsible for the activities of all assigned Floor Trainers and should be ready and willing to help with those on other Floor Trainer Teams. Team Leads support Training Management in implementation of corrective actions to eliminate program compliance issues after training. Team Leads may assist in the facilitation of training materials and programs, as needed. Team Leads maintain Floor Support records and files. Team Leads ensure Operations staff adherence to Standard Operating Procedures (SOP's) and training requirements, including new procedure training and up-training activities. Team Leads report all Floor Support Team needs to Training Management. Team Leads must also meet and fulfill the duties and responsibilities of Floor Trainers.

FLOOR SUPPORT SHIFT LEAD

Shift Leads are responsible for the supporting, coaching, and leading of Team Leads and other assigned Floor Trainers. Shift Leads partner with Team Leads and Operations staff to ensure training compliance is met. Shift Leads collaborate with Floor

Support Staff to meet training goals and implement operational changes to enhance effectiveness. Shift Leads communicate all training updates and ensure Team Leads are aware of and implementing updates with their teams. Shift Leads oversee and coordinate the work of Team Leads throughout the Business Operations. Shift Leads are responsible for the activities of all assigned Team Leads. Shift Leads may assist in the facilitation of training materials and programs, as needed. Shift Leads maintain Floor Support records and files. Shift Leads report all Floor Support Team needs to Training Management. Shift Leads must also meet and fulfill the duties and responsibilities of Team Leads and Floor Trainers, as needed.

FLOOR SUPPORT FLOOR LEAD

The Floor Lead is responsible for the overall strategy and execution of the Floor Support program focusing on excellent educational experiences and process compliance. The Floor Lead is responsible for establishing a Floor Training system and team that promotes company goals and objectives, and positively impacts active production Customer Service Representative Performance. The Floor Lead champions continuous improvement efforts and compliance initiatives including initiating and implementing training and development activities as appropriate. The Floor Lead oversees the education and training of active production Managers,

Supervisors and Customer Service Representatives. The Floor Lead works to fulfill company objectives by providing leadership in educational development, planning, coordinating, staffing, and training under the guidance of the Training Supervisor. The Floor Lead must also meet and fulfill the duties and responsibilities of Floor Leads, Team Leads and Floor Trainers, as needed.

CCO TRAINER

The Communications and Current Operations (CCO) Trainer is responsible to serve as an advocate for Floor Support to build and sustain positive relations with employees and the company. The CCO Trainer is responsible for creating releases that contain important updates from Business Operations to remain up-to-date and provide materials that will help team members excel in their positions. The CCO Trainer will act as a liaison for the Training Supervisor to ensure policies are being followed correctly according to company standard operating procedures. The CCO Trainer promotes company goals and objectives and positively impacts Customer Service Representative Performance through memorandums or other means of communication. The CCO Trainer provides material that follows the guidelines from the company by not creating material that would be contrary to the direction given by management. The CCO Trainer will thoroughly learn any new curriculum and train the Floor Support team on the new material.

The CCO Trainer will assist the Floor Lead in initiating and implementing training and development activities as appropriate. The CCO Trainer must also meet and fulfill the duties and responsibilities of Floor Leads, Team Leads and Floor Trainers, as needed.

INDIVIDUAL DEVELOPMENT PLANS

To assure the organization has improvement on a continual basis the Individual Development Plan was created. We have found (as many before us) that measuring performance helps an individual (and an organization) to see growth and areas for improvement. The Individual Development Plan (IDP) has been established with the intent of helping every team member to grow. The plans themselves are as individualized as the individuals who undertake them, but there are forms used to help in that process. The goal is to drive leadership development. This is in keeping with the aforementioned Career Development Plan and its inherent structure. IDPs can be monitored and tracked as a measure of progress, used as a way to drive accountability for development, and most importantly, if they take seriously, they really do work in producing leadership.

There are four different forms to use in the maintenance of Individual Development Plans:

- **Floor Trainer Evaluation** – this form is used with team members to evaluate their floor support activities, specifically: accessibility, communication of knowledge, and leadership presence. There is no scoring matrix for this form as of yet. This should be done based on team size (e.g. a team of 10 or below would be weekly, a team of 10-20+ would be bi-weekly).

- **Classroom Trainer Evaluation** – this form is used with team members to evaluate their classroom skills, specifically: preparation, presentation skills, communication of knowledge, and classroom management. This includes a scoring matrix. This should be done based on team size (e.g. a team of 10 or below would be weekly, a team of 10-20+ would be bi-weekly).
- **Short Performance Evaluation** – this is a shorter form to be done every 90 days to help keep tabs on growth and goals with each team member. This is meant for understanding overall performance, specifically: job knowledge, deliverable production, written communication, initiative, communication/listening skills, accessibility/dependability, and an overall rating of performance.
- **Observation Documentation Form** – this form is used for documenting both good and poor performance incidents and one-on-ones. This kind of documentation is expected to be done on a weekly basis, preferably 2 times a week.

OBSERVATION DOCUMENTATION FORM

Employee:	Job Title:
Date:	Date/Time of Incident:
Time:	Location of Incident:
Policy Violated (if applicable):	Team Lead:
Description of Incident:	
Employee Statement:	
Supervisor Comments:	

```
Action Taken:




```

After there is structure and purpose, the tools for a continuous improvement culture need to be implemented. We've developed two different reports that will help in developing the kinds of habits necessary to keep moving forward as an organization.

There are two different, essential forms to use on a daily/semi-daily basis by Floor Trainers:

- **Daily Shift Report** – this report tracks information on a general level for the end-of-shift; this helps to track daily trends, especially concerning production floor moral and the Floor Support actions necessary to improve production each day.
- **Daily Process Observations** – this report is for tracking every interaction with a CSR, Supervisor, Manager, etc. in order to track trends on a moment-to-moment basis.

Below are copies of the different reports.

DAILY SHIFT REPORT

Directions: Answer the following questions – it's as simple as that.

TIME SPENT

In percentages, how much time did you spend with the following CSRs?

PHONE: _____   WEB CHAT: _____

EXAMPLE OF A CSR THAT WAS HELPED AND HOW THEY WERE HELPED

EXAMPLE OF A CSR THAT WAS HELPED AND HOW THEY WERE HELPE

STATEMENT OF MORALE ON THE FLOOR AT *START OF SHIFT*

STATEMENT OF MORALE ON THE FLOOR AT *END OF SHIFT*

Action Statement

How did you help improve production for the day?

DAILY PROCESS OBSERVATIONS

Directions: To better understand both individual and team needs, please fill out the following form.

TODAY'S TOPIC:

_____

CSR:

SUPERVISOR:

Correct processes followed? Yes _____ No _____
Explain:

CSR:

SUPERVISOR:

Correct processes followed? Yes _____ No _____
Explain:

CSR:

     SUPERVISOR:

Correct processes followed? Yes _____ No _____
Explain:

CSR:

     SUPERVISOR:

Correct processes followed? Yes _____ No _____
Explain:

CLASS ROOM DEVELOPMENT

During times when Floor Support needs to adapt to
Classroom Trainings (in those cases where Floor
Support is developed out of the training group), the
structure still stands from Shift Lead on up, but the
organization modifies to match the needs of
classroom training. Floor Support Trainers must be
adaptable according to the needs of the company.
This adaptability includes when CCO Trainer, Floor
Lead, and Shift Leads need to be part of the
classroom trainings. When this happens, Shift Leads
are absorbed into the training groups as needed,
followed by the Floor Lead and CCO Trainer. In these
cases, titles shift from being Floor Support to
Classroom Support (e.g. Classroom Trainer,
Classroom Team Lead, Classroom Training Shift

Lead, etc.). For further details, see the 'Classroom Support Job Descriptions' section below.

As with Floor Support, these job descriptions lend clarity to responsibilities and expectations and also give purpose and direction to the learning experience necessary for true continuous improvement.

CLASSROOM SUPPORT JOB DESCRIPTIONS

CLASSROOM TRAINER

Classroom Trainers leverage knowledge and relationships to understand the training and development needs of customer service personnel and work to meet those needs through support, individual coaching, and team trainings. Classroom Trainers are responsible for building positive relationships with Managers, Supervisors and Customer Service Representatives. Classroom Trainers draft reports and communicate findings and analysis with Training Management. Classroom Trainers perform day-to-day delivery, administration, interpretation and compliance of learning programs according to established policies and procedures. Classroom Trainers support the continuous improvement of their functional area through development and implementation of learning programs. With guidance, Classroom Trainers provide expertise, support and advice to Managers,

Supervisors and Customer Service Representatives and other management teams. Classroom Trainers serve on cross functional teams and share best practices. Classroom Trainers conduct Root Cause Analysis and Needs Assessments.

CLASSROOM TRAINING TEAM LEAD

Team Leads are responsible for supporting, coaching, and leading a team of Classroom Trainers. Team Leads partner with Operations Support Staff to ensure training compliance is met. Team Leads collaborate with classroom training staff to meet training goals and implement operational changes to enhance effectiveness. Team Leads continuously train Classroom Trainers on all training updates. Team Leads conduct, direct and lead training and related developmental activities needed to support operational objectives in support of the Operations Support Staff and Training Management. Team Leads oversee and coordinate the work of assigned Classroom Trainers throughout the Business Operations. Team Leads are responsible for the activities of all assigned Classroom Trainers and should be ready and willing to help with those on other Classroom Trainer Teams. Team Leads support Training Management in implementation of corrective actions to eliminate program compliance issues after training. Team Leads may assist in the facilitation of training materials and programs, as needed. Team Leads maintain Classroom Training records and files.

Team Leads ensure Operations Staff adherence to Standard Operating Procedures (SOP's) and training requirements, including new procedure training and up-training activities. Team Leads report all Classroom Training Team needs to Training Management. Team Leads must also meet and fulfill the duties and responsibilities of Classroom Trainers.

CLASSROOM TRAINING SHIFT LEAD

Shift Leads are responsible for the supporting, coaching, and leading of Team Leads and other assigned Classroom Trainers. Shift Leads partner with Team Leads and Operations Support Staff to ensure training compliance is met. Shift Leads collaborate with Classroom Training staff to meet training goals and implement operational changes to enhance effectiveness. Shift Leads communicate all training updates and ensure Team Leads are aware of and implementing updates with their teams. Shift Leads oversee and coordinate the work of Team Leads throughout the Business Operations Staff. Shift Leads are responsible for the activities of all assigned Team Leads. Shift Leads may assist in the facilitation of training materials and programs, as needed. Shift Leads maintain Classroom Training records and files. Shift Leads report all Classroom Training Team needs to Training Management. Shift Leads must also meet and fulfill the duties and responsibilities of Team Leads and Classroom Trainers, as needed.

CLASSROOM TRAINING LEAD

The Classroom Lead is responsible for the overall strategy and execution of the Classroom Training program focusing on excellent educational experiences and process compliance. The Classroom Lead is responsible for establishing a Classroom Training system (as needed) and team that promotes company goals and objectives, and positively impacts Customer Service Representative Performance. The Classroom Lead champions continuous improvement efforts and compliance initiatives including initiating and implementing training and development activities as appropriate. The Classroom Lead oversees the education and training of Managers, Supervisors and Customer Service Representatives. The Classroom Lead works to fulfill company objectives by providing leadership in educational development, planning, coordinating, staffing, and training under the guidance of the Training Supervisor. The Classroom Lead must also meet and fulfill the duties and responsibilities of Shift Leads, Team Leads and Classroom Trainers, as needed.

CCO TRAINER (CLASSROOM SUPPORT)

The Communications and Current Operations (CCO) Trainer is responsible to serve as an advocate for Floor Support to build and sustain positive relations with employees and the company. The CCO Trainer is responsible for creating releases that contain important updates from Business Operations to remain up-to-date and provide materials that will help team members excel in their positions. The CCO Trainer will act as a liaison for the Training Supervisor to ensure policies are being followed correctly according to company standard operating procedures. The CCO Trainer promotes company goals and objectives and positively impacts Customer Service Representative Performance through memorandums or other means of communication. The CCO Trainer provides material that follows the guidelines from the company by not creating material that would be contrary to the direction given by management. The CCO Trainer will thoroughly learn any new curriculum and train the Floor Support team on the new material.

The CCO Trainer will assist the Floor Lead in initiating and implementing training and development activities as appropriate. The CCO Trainer must also meet and fulfill the duties and responsibilities of Floor Leads, Team Leads and Floor Trainers, as needed.

ACCOUNTABILITY

There is no use in all of these developmental steps for individuals and continuous improvement for the organization as a whole if there is no accountability. A culture is only as good as what we measure and what we reward and/or punish. To focus the efforts of your staff, set boundaries.

Accountability means that individuals are not only responsible for something but also ultimately answerable for their actions. Developing a culture built around accountability, not with punishment in mind but with a desire to learn from experience, gives ownership over one's experience in this life. In order to have the most impact from emotional physics, we must be learning and helping each other to learn. Therefore, we need to put accountability in place and then be consistent in keeping that accountability going.

A basic principle of accountability in a workplace is attendance. The following example policy is one that we have used with much success. It's simple and works for a multiplicity of environments. When it comes to a customer service environment, this has been especially helpful in keeping track of who is accountable for their attendance and punctuality and who is not, without producing a culture of micromanagement. As with all things, you can decide how to implement such a policy, but we advise that you have a policy, regardless.

EXAMPLE ATTENDANCE AND PUNCTUALITY POLICY

As an employee of a [company], we expect you to be reliable and punctual by reporting to work on time and as scheduled. When you are absent or late, it places a burden on other employees and can impact productivity and service.

- In the rare instances when you cannot avoid being late or are unable to work as scheduled, you must notify your supervisor as soon as possible so that appropriate arrangements can be made. If your supervisor is not available, contact any other management personnel from your department. Please do not leave a message on a voice mail machine or with a fellow employee.

- If your absence lasts more than one day, you must report your absence daily unless other arrangements have been made with your supervisor. Additionally, if you are going to be off work due to illness for more than 3 consecutive days, a physician's note may be required.

All additional Time-Off Requests for sick time must be approved by the Human Resources Department. Employees will be required to use all accrued Paid Time-Off before being allowed to take any approved unpaid absences.

3 consecutive days of 'No Call No Show' (not calling in and absent) is considered voluntary termination and will result in the employee forfeiting their employment with [company].

Unplanned absences, a poor attendance record, frequent tardiness and failure to call in when absent cause disruptions in work. This may lead to disciplinary action, up to and including termination of employment.

POINT SYSTEM

The Point System is designed to take the consequence of missing work off the shoulders of management and put it back on the employee. This in turn put the employee in control of their future with the [company]. The Point System structure is as follows.
- Each employee starts with 12 points.
- Each 30 day period (from the last attendance incident) that is attended with no absences or other infractions, the employee will accrue 0.5 points back into their account.
- The max amount of points that can be accumulated (in total) is 15.
- If an employee calls in sick they will lose 1 point.
- If an employee is tardy (going to be late) and does not communicate the tardy previous to their being late they will lose 0.5 points.
- If you are going to be off work due to illness for more than 3 consecutive days, a physician's note will be required. Each consecutive day the employee must use normal call-in procedures (only 1 point will be accrued in this case).

- If the normal call in procedure is not followed the employee will accrue 3 points for each consecutive day missed.
- If an employee does not call in and is absent (No Call No Show or 'NCNS') then each day is worth 3 points.
- If an employee has to leave early without prior consent, they will lose 0.5 points.

GUIDE LINES FOR DISCIPLINARY ACTION

- Any team member reaching a balance of 5 points will get a verbal warning.
- Any team member reaching a balance of 3 points will get a written warning.
- Any team member reaching a balance of 1 point will get a final warning.
- Any team member reaching a balance of 0 points may be terminated.

POINT ALLOCATION

Situation

Situation	Points
Each employee will start with a balance of	12
Each month that is attended with no absences or other infractions the employee will accrue	0.5
The max amount of points that can be accumulated	15
If an employee calls in sick they will lose	1
If an employee is tardy (going to be late) and does not communicate the tardy previous to	

their being late they will lose	0.5
If you are going to be off work due to illness for more than 3 consecutive days, a physician's note will be required. Each consecutive day the employee must use normal call-in procedures. The employee will only lose	1
If the normal call in procedure is not followed the employee will accrue per day	3
If an employee does not call in and is absent (No Call No Show or 'NCNS') then each day is worth	3
If an employee has to leave early without prior consent, they will lose	0.5

Action

Points	Action
5	Verbal Warning
3	Written Warning
1	Final Warning
0	Termination

SOME FINAL THOUGHTS

In the business world, some things are different based on the type of business. Prior to the working year, management sits down with the employee in a one on one session and together they set goals that should be accomplished each year. At the end of the year, typically on the anniversary date of the employee, there is a review process that takes place. This is where management decides, based on the subsequent quarterly reviews, how well the employee has accomplished their goals and lived up to the company's goals and mission statement. In some companies performance increases are included within this process. It is important that the review not be biased in any way, even if there is a company mandated set amount that has been decided on for each employee's increase. If not, the manager could find themselves on one side of the table trying to convince the employee what he or she is worth, thus degrading the integrity of the process.

The integrity of these processes is only as good as those who are assigned to use these tools. They have been proven over the years to work and work well when used properly. In the classroom setting many have graduated as better students then when first started. In the business world all biases need to be put aside along with personal agendas. We must be about improving ourselves as an organization – our heart and soul there for all involved. From this, continued success will be the norm and integrity will dictate our future leaders.

www.ingramcontent.com/pod-product-compliance
Lightning Source LLC
Chambersburg PA
CBHW051253170526
45165CB00004B/1696